Follow the Lamb

Horatius Bonar

Christian Focus Publications Ltd

Published by
Christian Focus Publications Ltd
Geanies House
Fearn, Tain
Ross-shire IV20 1TW
Scotland

This edition 1987
ISBN 0 906731 63 1

Contents

Introduction

It is for you who are called by the name of Christ that these pages are written, that you may be reminded of what God expects of you, and of what your name commits you to.

It is a great thing to be a Christian. The very name is a noble one, beyond all the noble names of earth. The thing itself is inconceivably blessed and glorious. To say, 'I am a Christian,' is to say, 'I belong to God's nobility; I am of the peerage of heaven.'

Much, then, is expected of you. Do not disgrace the old family name. Do nothing unworthy of Him who represents you in heaven, and whom you represent on earth. He is faithful to you; be you so to Him. Let men know what a Lord and Master you serve. Be His witnesses; be His mirrors; be His living epistles. Let Him speak through you to the world; and do you speak of Him. Let your life tell your fellow-men what He is, and what He is to you. Speak well of Him to men, as He speaks well of you to God. He has honoured you by giving you His name; He has blessed you by conferring on you sonship, and royalty, and an eternal heritage: see that you do justice to His love, and magnify His greatness.

Let your light shine. Do not obstruct it, or hide it, or mingle darkness with it. 'Arise, shine; for thy light is come, and the glory of the Lord is risen upon thee' (*Isa. 60, v. 1*).

It is the light of *love* that you have received; let it shine. It is the light of *truth*; let it shine. It is the light of *holiness*; let it shine. And if you ask, How am I to get the light, and to maintain it in fulness? I answer, 'Christ shall give you light' (*Eph. 5, v. 14*). There is light enough in Him who is the light of the world. 'The Lamb is the light thereof' (*Rev. 21, v. 23*). There is no light for man but from the Lamb. It is the cross, the cross alone, that lights up a dark soul and keeps it shining, so that we walk in light as He is in the light; 'for God is light, and in Him is no darkness at all.'

Be true to Him who loved you, and washed you from your sins in His own blood. He deserves it at your hands. It is the least that you can do for Him.

Follow Him. His first words to you were, 'Come to me.' You came and found rest. But He adds these two other messages, 'Abide in me,' and 'Follow me.' You take up your cross as He took up His; and you follow Him. You go forth without the camp, bearing His reproach (*Luke 9, v. 23; Heb. 13, v. 13*). Through good report and through bad report you follow Him. He draws you, leads you, keeps you — and so you follow Him. Your whole life is to be one continuous following of the Lord. 'If any man serve me, let him *follow* me; and where I am, there shall also my servant be: if any man serve me, him will my Father honour' (*John 12, v. 26*). 'My sheep hear my voice, and they *follow* me' (*John 10, v. 27*). '*Followers* of Him who is good' is Peter's description of a believing man (*1 Pet. 3, v. 13*); such is the proper rendering of the passage, and not 'of that which is good'. And the sure promise is, 'He that followeth me shall not walk in darkness, but shall have the light of life' (*John 8, v. 12*).

In following Him, you will look *onward*; for He set His face stedfastly to go up to Jerusalem; and when Peter would have hindered His going to the cross, He answered, 'Get thee behind me, Satan' (*Matt. 16, v. 23*). You will look *upward* too; for He 'lifted up His eyes to heaven;' and your posture must be 'looking upwards,' with your affection set on things above (*Col. 3, v. 1*). You must bear the contradiction of sinners as He did (*Heb. 12, v. 3*); you must count the reproach of Christ greater riches than all earthly treasures (*Heb. 11, v. 26*); you must keep before your eyes Him who was 'despised and rejected of men,' yet who was 'meek and lowly in heart,' whose 'heart was not haughty nor His eyes lofty, who did not exercise Himself in great matters or in things too high for Him, who behaved and quieted Himself as a child that is weaned of his mother, whose soul was as a weaned child' (*Ps. 131, vv. 1, 2*).

You began with turning your back upon the world, and 'looking to Jesus;' keep ever thus. Looking to Him brought rest to you at first, and healed your soul; so, looking to Him daily will maintain your rest and perfect your spiritual health. 'Looking to Jesus' will give you light in hours of darkness, will strengthen you in weakness, will comfort you in trouble, will cheer you in the day of weariness. Should your eye ever be withdrawn from the cross, you will be sure to go back, to grow cold, and to forget that you were purged from your old sins (*2 Pet. 1, v. 9*). That cross is life, health, holiness, consolation, strength, joy; let nothing come between it and you. In the light of that cross go upon your way stedfastly; for to him on whose path that cross is shining, there can be no abiding darkness.

Clouds there may be and eclipses; but that light can never be quenched; that sun can never go down.

Remember what you are, and what God expects at your hand. Act out your own professions, your own faith, your own prayers.

God has had mercy on you; and in His great love he has laid His almighty hand on you that you might be saved. He has 'sent from above, and taken, and drawn you out of many waters' (*Ps. 12, v. 16*); delivering you not only 'from the wrath to come' (*1 Thess. 1, v. 10*), but from 'a present evil world' (*Gal. 1, v. 4*). By His gracious power He has turned you from the error of your ways; and one of the many names by which you are henceforth to be known on earth is that of 'converts' or 'turned ones.'

But your 'turning' or 'conversion' is only a beginning; no more. It is not the whole; it is but the first step. You are a 'disciple,' that is, one under teaching; but your teaching, your discipleship, has only *commenced*. Your life is a Book; it may be a volume of larger or smaller size; and conversion is but the title-page or the preface. The Book itself remains to be written; and your years and weeks and days are its chapters and leaves and lines. It is a Book written for eternity; see that it be written well. It is a Book for the inspection of enemies as well as friends; be careful of every word. It is a Book written under the eye of God; let it be done reverently; without levity, yet without constraint or terror.

Let me give you a few counsels. You will soon feel your need of them, unless, perhaps, you are of those who are too wise to learn, and are 'vainly puffed up in their fleshly mind.'

Chapter 1

Be strong in the grace that is in Christ Jesus

It was this grace or free love which first began with you, and with which you began. It was this which you at first 'apprehended,' or rather, which 'apprehended' you; and your special character is that of men who 'know the grace of God' (*Col. 1, v. 6*); who have 'tasted that the Lord is gracious' (*1 Pet. 2, v. 3*); men on whom God has had compassion (*Rom. 9, v. 15*); men to whom He has showed His forgiving love. Such is your name.

This grace of God is your strength, as it is your joy; and it is only by abiding in it that you can really live the life of the redeemed. Be strong, then, in this grace; draw your joy out of it; and beware how you turn to anything else for refreshment, or comfort, or holiness. Though a believing man, you are still a sinner; a sinner to the last; and, as such, nothing can suit you but the free love of God. Be strong in it. Remember that you are saved by believing, not by doubting. Be not then a doubter, but a believer. Draw continually on Christ and His fulness for this grace. If at any time you are beguiled away from it, return to it without delay; and betake yourself to it again just as you did at the first. To recover lost peace, go back to where you got it at first; begin your spiritual life all over again: get at once to the resting-place. Where sin has abounded, let grace much more abound. Do not go back to your feelings, or

experiences, or evidences, in order to extract from
them a renewal of your lost peace. Go straight back to
the free love of God. You found peace in it at first; you
will find peace in it to the last. This was the *beginning*
of your confidence; let it be both last and first.

This abounding grace, rightly understood, will not
make you sin; it will not relax morality or make
inconsistency a trifle. It will magnify sin and enhance
its evil in your eyes. Your footing or 'standing' in grace
(*Rom. 5, v 2*) will be the strongest, as well as most
blessed, that you can ever occupy. If your feet be 'shod
with the preparation of the gospel of peace' (*Eph. 6, v.
15*), you will be able to 'stand' and to 'withstand;' not
otherwise. Remember how Paul and Barnabas urged
this upon the Jews of Antioch, 'persuading them to
continue in *the grace* of God' (*Acts 13, v. 43; Gal. 5, v.
4; Tit. 2, v. 11; 1 Pet. 5, v. 12*).

Chapter 2

Keep the conscience clean

When you first saw the *cross*, and understood the meaning of the *blood*, you got your conscience 'purged from dead works' (*Heb. 9, v. 14*); and it was this cleansing of the conscience that gave you peace. It was not that you ceased to be a sinner, or lost the *consciousness* of being one, but you had found something which pacified your conscience in a righteous way, and made you feel towards the law and the Lawgiver just as if you had never been guilty.

It is by keeping constantly before your eyes this blood of propitiation that you will keep your conscience clean and your soul at peace. It is this blood alone that can wipe off the continual sins that are coming across your conscience, and which, if not wiped off *immediately*, will effectually stain it, and cloud your peace. You know how the steel of the finest sword may be rusted by a drop of water. Yet if the water is not allowed to remain, but is wiped away as soon as it falls, it harms not the steel, and no rust ensues. If, however, through neglect or otherwise, the water is allowed to remain, rust will follow, destroying both the edge and brightness of the weapon. So is it with sin. The moment it falls upon the conscience, the blood must be applied; else dimness and doubting will be the consequence. Remember it is the *blood*, the *blood alone*; that can remove these.

If, when you sin, you do not go at once to this and be washed and pardoned, but betake yourself to anything else first, you will only make bad worse. If you shrink from going *directly* to Christ and His blood; if you try to slip gradually near in some roundabout way, as if you hoped, by the time you reach the fountain, to get quit of part of the sin, so as not to be quite so bad as at the moment when you committed it, you will not cleanse the conscience, but leave the burden and the stain just where they were. If you say, 'But I am so ruffled with the sin, so cast down and ashamed at the thought of what I have done, that I dare *not* go at once to the blood; I must pray or read myself into a better frame, and *then* I will go and be washed;' you are denying God's method of purging the conscience; you are undervaluing the blood; you are reverting to your old ways of self-righteousness; and you are preventing the restoration of lost peace; for you are putting something between your conscience and the blood.

Keep, then, the conscience clean by continual application to the blood; and you will find that this, instead of encouraging you to sin, will make you more ashamed and afraid of it, than if you had got quit of it in some self-righteous way of your own. What more likely to make you fear and hate it than being compelled to go with it constantly to God, and deal with Him directly about its pardon?

Cultivate a *tender* conscience; but beware of a *diseased* and *morbid* one. The former takes an honest, straightforward view of truth or duty, and acts accordingly. The latter, overlooking what is broad and great, is always on the hunt for trifles, quibbling and questioning about things of no importance. Thus a stiff

Christianity is produced, an artificial religion, very unlike the erect but easy walk of one who possesses the liberty of Christ. Be natural, be simple, be easy in word and manner, lest you seem as one acting a part. Cherish a free spirit, a large heart, and a clear conscience, like the apostle, who, though he pitied the 'weaker brethren' (*1 Cor. 8, vv. 9-13*), refused to allow his liberty in Christ to be narrowed by another man's morbid conscience. Certainly beware of *little* sins; but be sure that they are sins. Omit no *little* duties; but see that they are duties. A tender and tranquil conscience does not make a man crotchety or troublesome, far less morose and supercilious; it makes him frank, cheerful, brotherly, and obliging, in the family, in the shop, in the congregation, in the market-place, whether he be poor or rich; so that others cannot help seeing how pleasantly he goes out and comes in, 'eating his meat with gladness and singleness of heart' (*Acts 2, v 46*), and so 'adorning the doctrine of God his Saviour in all things' (*Tit. 2, v. 10*).

Chapter 3

Hold fast that which you have received

Beware of changeableness; be not carried about with diverse and strange doctrines: it is a bad sign of a man when he is frequently shifting his ground and adopting new opinions. 'It is a good thing that the heart be *established* with grace' (*Heb. 13, v. 9*); and it is good to hold the beginning of our confidence stedfast unto the end (*Heb. 3, v. 14*). The 'righteousness of God' was that which you began with, and you found it an ample covering and a sufficient resting-place. God's reckoning your sin to Christ, and His righteousness to you, was joy and peace, when you found the burden of your grief too great for you to bear. Never let go your hold of this truth. Continue to rejoice in this blessed exchange. Let the righteousness of the Righteous One be your daily covering.

When a man gets wearied of what is old, and is always catching hold of what is new, it looks as if he had been beguiled from the simplicity that is in Christ, and had lost his relish for the things of Christ; nay, almost as if he had never been 'rooted and grounded in love.' Love of *novelties* has been the shipwreck of many a soul. 'Some new thing' is the craving not of the men of Athens only, but of many in the Church of God. They are restless; and are carried about with diverse and strange doctrines. Old truths get tame and stale (*Eph. 4, v. 14*; *Heb. 13, v. 9*; *1 John 4, v. 1*). Take care of 'itching ears' (*2 Tim. 4, v. 3*), and of 'heaping to yourselves teachers' (*2 Tim. 4, v. 3*).

Along with this we often see the love of *controversy*, which is almost equally pernicious, even when it takes the side of truth. The man who likes better to be fighting about his food than eating it, is likely to remain lean enough. Disputes, like offences, must sometimes come; but, like David's 'sharp razor' (*Ps. 52, v. 2*), they 'work deceitfully,' and are difficult to handle safely. They often eat out *love*, even when they do not destroy *faith*. Yet cleave to the truth; nay, if error does assail you, 'contend earnestly for the faith once delivered to the saints;' 'that which ye have already, hold fast, that no man take thy crown.' Satan, either as the prince of darkness or as an angel of light, resist, 'stedfast in the faith.' Don't dally with error, and don't tamper with truth. 'Buy the truth' (*Prov. 23, v. 23*) at any price; but 'sell it not' for all the gold and silver on earth. And while you are on your guard against errors and changes, beware of *excitement*. The 'mind that was in Christ' is *calm*, not restless and ruffled; the work of the Spirit is to *calm*, not to excite; and the tendency of the Gospel, as well as of all Bible truth, is to *calm*, not to agitate. Do not use strong language, and startling phrases, and wild images, which are fitted to make others shudder. The Spirit of God is not in the fire, or the earthquake, or the hurricane; but in the still, small voice. Beware of sensationalism either in religious experience, or in the statement of facts, or in the exposition of truth. That which is merely emotional or sentimental, not only dies down, but often leaves insensibility, if not a seared conscience behind it. The

Master was always calm: calmness is true strength, or at least it is the result of strength. As an overpowering gale keeps down the waters over which it is rushing, so true intensity of spiritual feeling does not show itself by loud vociferations, but by the depth and solemnity of the calm which it diffuses through the soul, and utters in brief-spoken words of tranquil simplicity.

Yet do not believe all that you hear from worldly men or half-hearted Christians about the 'excitement' attending revivals. Conversion is not excitement; zeal is not excitement; love for souls is not excitement; trembling under the word is not excitement; and even if there be some excitement at 'revival meetings,' better that it should be so than that souls should perish. There is more excitement in the theatre and the ball-room, or the concert, or the political meeting, or the parliamentary election, or even what is called the 'quiet evening party.' Yet men do not complain of these, nor get angry at them. By all means be calm; but don't suppose that all excitement is sin or hypocrisy. Excitement is not good; but some things are worse than even this. A dull and sleepy Christianity is worse — much worse; a stiff and frozen formalism is worse — much worse; an easy-minded worldly religion is worse — much worse. It is a good thing to be 'zealously affected always' (*Gal. 4, v. 18*); and to be 'fervent in spirit' (*Rom. 12, v. 11*). 'Whatsoever thy hand findeth to do, do it with thy might' (*Eccles. 9, v. 10*). If it is worth doing at all, do it well; throw your soul into it, 'do it heartily' (*Col. 3, v. 23*).

Chapter 4

Deal honestly with yourselves

'If we would judge ourselves, we should not be judged' (*1 Cor. 11, v. 31*); *i.e.* if we would but faithfully judge ourselves, we should be spared the infliction of divine chastisements. But we are not faithful to our own souls. We deal with a slack hand in things pertaining to our own sins, and let things go unreproved and uncondemned in ourselves which we are sharp enough to discover and rebuke in others. Deal honestly with every part of your daily life; in regard to duty, or trial, or sacrifice, or self-denial, or forbearance with others. Beware of *onesidedness* or self-partiality — in truth, in experience, or in action. Remember that all things have two sides: a tender conscience and a well-balanced mind will deal with both. Deal honestly with conscience in all things, small and great, spiritual or temporal; deal honestly with the Church of God, and with the brethren; deal honestly with God — Father, Son, and Spirit.

Strange that in spiritual things we should try to cheat *ourselves* as well as others! Yet so it is. We are loath to take the worst view of our own case; to think evil of ourselves; to act the stern censor in regard to our own omissions and commissions. We have few excuses for others, many for ourselves; evils that seem monstrous in others are trifles in us. When looking at others, we use a microscope; at ourselves, we either shut our eyes or put on a veil. This dishonest dealing is very pernicious; this 'covering of sin' is destructive both of peace and progress. And when we remember that all dishonest dealing with ourselves is in reality dishonest dealing with God, the evil is seen to be the more hateful and the more inexcusable (*Hos. 11, v. 12*). Be honest and upright before God and man; with your own conscience; with the blood of sprinkling; and with that law which is 'holy, and just, and good.' Don't flatter your own heart, nor tell a lie to conscience, nor think to deceive God (*Ps. 101, v. 7; Jer. 9, v. 6, 17, v. 9; Gal. 6, v. 3; Jas. 1, v. 22; 1 John 1, v. 8*).

Chapter 5

Keep company with God, and with the people of God

Intimacy with God is the very essence of religion, and the foundation of discipleship. It is in intercourse with Father, Son, and Spirit that the most *real* parts of our lives are lived; and all parts that are not lived in fellowship with Him, 'in whom we live, and move, and have our being,' are *unreal*, untrue, unsuccessful, and unsatisfying. The understanding of doctrine is one thing, and intimacy with God is another. They ought always to go together; but they are often seen asunder; and, when there is the former without the latter, there is a hard, proud, hollow religion. Get your teaching from God (*Job 36, v. 22; Jer. 23, v. 30*); take your doctrine from His lips; learn truth upon your knees. Beware of opinions and speculations: they become idols, and nourish pride of intellect; they furnish no food to the soul; they make you sapless and heartless; they are like winter frost-work on your windowpane, shutting out the warm sun.

Let God be your companion, your bosom-friend, your instructor, your counsellor. Take Him into the closet with you, into the study, into the shop, into the market-place, into the railway carriage, into the boat. When you make a feast and call guests, invite Him as one of them. He is always willing to come; and there is no company like His. When you are in perplexity, and are taking advice from friends, let Him be one of your 'friends in council.' When you feel lonely, make Him the 'companion of your solitude.' And if you are known to be one given to the divine companionship, you will be saved from much idle and wasteful society and conversation. You will not feel at home with worldly men, nor they with you. You will not choose the half-and-half Christian, or the formalist, or the servant of two masters, for your friend; nor will any of these seek your fellowship. When thrown into worldly society, from your business or your relationships, as you may sometimes be, do not cease to be the Christian; nor try to make excuses for the worldliness of those with whom you are obliged to associate; for that is just making excuses for yourself in associating with them. Do not try to make yourself or them believe that they are religious when they are not; but show them whose disciples you are; not necessarily in words, but by a line of conduct more expressive and efficacious than words. Do not conform to the world in order to please men or to save yourself from their taunt or jest. Be not afraid to ask a blessing at meals, or to have family worship, or to enter into religious conversation, because a worldly man is present. Keep constant company with the great God of heaven and earth; and let every other companionship be regulated by His. Go where you please, if you can take Him with you; go nowhere if He cannot be admitted, or if you are obliged for the time to conceal or disguise your divine discipleship. When Joseph went down to Egypt, he took the young child with him (*Matt. 2, v. 21*); so, wherever you go, take the young child with you.

Beware of declension in prayer. — Whenever you feel the closet becoming a *dull* place, you may be sure that there is something wrong. Backsliding has begun. Go straight to God that He may 'heal it' (*Hos. 14, v. 4*). Do not trifle with it; nor resort to other expedients to relieve the dullness, such as shortening the time, or getting some lively religious books to take off the weariness; go at once to the Great Quickener with the cry, 'Quicken us, and we will call on Thy name' (*Ps. 80, v. 18*). Beware of going through prayer in a careless or perfunctory way, like a hireling doing his work in order to get done with it. 'Pray in the Holy Ghost' (*Jude v. 20*). 'Pray without ceasing.' Pray with honest fervour and simple faith, as men who really want what they ask for, and expect to get it all. Few things tend more to deaden the soul, to harden the heart, to drive out spirituality, than cold, formal prayer. It will eat as doth a canker. Dread it and shun it. Do not mock God by asking what you don't want, or by pretending to desire what you don't care for. 'The end of all things is at hand; be ye therefore sober, and watch unto prayer' (*1 Pet. 4, v. 7*).

Be much alone with God. Do not put Him off with a quarter of an hour morning and evening. Take time to get thoroughly acquainted. Converse over everything with Him. Unbosom yourself wholly — every thought, feeling, wish, plan, doubt — to Him. He wants converse with His creatures; shall His creatures not want converse with Him? He wants, not merely to be on 'good terms' with you, if one may use man's phrase, but to be *intimate*; shall you decline the intimacy, and be satisfied with mere acquaintance? What! intimate with the world, with friends, with neigh-

bours, with politicians, with philosophers, with natur-
alists, or with poets; but not with God! That would
look ill indeed. Folly, to prefer the clay to the potter,
the marble to the sculptor, this little earth and its lesser
creatures to the mighty Maker of the universe, the great
'All and in all!'

Do not shrink from being alone. Much of a true
man's true life must be so spent. David Brainerd thus
writes:— 'My state of solitude does not make the hours
hang heavy upon my hands. Oh, what reason of
thankfulness have I on account of this retirement! I find
that I do not, and it seems I cannot, lead a Christian life
when I am abroad, and cannot spend time in devotion,
in conversation, and serious meditation, as I should do.
These weeks that I am obliged now to be from home, in
order to learn the Indian tongue, are mostly spent in
perplexity and barrenness, without much relish of
divine things; and I feel myself a stranger at the throne
of grace for want of a more frequent and continued
retirement.' Do not suppose that such retirement for
divine converse will hinder work. It will greatly help it.
Much private fellowship with God will give you seven-
fold success. Pray much if you would work much; and
if you want to work more, pray more. Luther used to
say, when an unusual press of business came upon him,
'I must pray *more* to-day.' Be like him in the day of
work or trial. Do not think that mere *working* will keep
you right or set you right. The watch won't go till the
spring is mended. Work will do nothing for you till *you
have gone to God for a working heart*. Trying to *work*
yourself into a better frame of feeling is not only
hopeless, but injurious. You say, I want to feel more
and to love more. It is well. But you can't work

yourself into these. I do not say to any one who feels his coldness, 'Go and *work*.' Work, if done heartlessly, will only make you colder. You must go straight to Jesus with that cold heart, and warm it at His cross; then work will be at once a necessity, a delight, and a success.

Chapter 6

Study the Bible

Do not skim it or read it, but *study* it, every word of it; study the whole Bible, Old Testament and New; not your favourite chapters merely, but the complete Word of God from beginning to end. Do not trouble yourself with commentators; they may be of use if kept in their place, but they are not your guides; your guide is 'the Interpreter,' the one among a thousand (*Job 33, v. 23*), who will lead you into all truth, and keep you from all error.

Not that you are to read no book but the Bible. All that is *true* and *good* is worth the reading, *if you have time for it*; and all, if properly used, will help you in your study of the Scriptures. A Christian does not shut his eyes to the natural scenes of beauty spread around him. He does not cease to admire the hills, or plains, or rivers, or forests of earth, because he has learned to love the God that made them; nor does he turn away from books of science or true poetry, because he has discovered one book truer, more precious, and more poetical than all the rest together. Besides, the soul can no more continue in one posture than the body. The eye must be relieved by variety of objects and the limbs by motion; so must the soul by change of subject and position. 'All truth is precious, though not all divine.'

In so far, then, as time allows or opportunity presents,

let us 'seek and search out by word concerning all things that are done under heaven.' But let the Bible be to us the book of books, the one book in all the world, whose every wisdom is truth, and whose every verse is wisdom. In studying it, be sure to take it for what it really is, the revelation of the *thoughts* of God given us in the *words* of God. Were it only the book of *divine* thoughts and *human* words, it would profit little, for we never could be sure whether the words really represented the thoughts; nay, we might be quite sure that man would fail in his *words* when attempting to embody divine *thoughts*; and that, therefore, if we have only man's words, that is, man's translation of the divine thoughts, we shall have one of the poorest and most incorrect of all books, just as we should have in the case of Homer or Plato done into English by a first year's schoolboy. But, knowing that we have *divine thoughts* embodied in *divine words*, through the inspiration of an unerring translator, we sit down to the study of the heavenly volume, assured that we shall find in all its teachings the perfection of wisdom, and in its language the *most accurate expression of that wisdom* that the finite speech of man can utter.

Every word of God is as perfect as it is pure (*Ps. 19, v. 7, 12, v. 6*). Let us read and re-read the Scriptures, meditating on them day and night. They never grow old, they never lose their sap, they never run dry. Though it is right and profitable, as I have said, to read other books, if they are true and good, yet beware of reading too many. Do not let man's book thrust God's book into a corner. Do not let commentaries smother the text; nor let the true and the good shut out the truer and the better.

Specially beware of light reading. *Shun novels*; they are the litarary curse of the age; they are to the soul what ardent spirits are to the body. If you be a parent, keep novels out of the way of your children. But whether you be a parent or not, neither read them yourself, nor set an example of novel-reading to others. Don't let novels lie on your table, or be seen in your hand, even in a railway carriage. The 'light reading for the rail' has done deep injury to many a young man and woman. The light literature of the day is working a world of harm; vitiating the taste of the young, enervating their minds, unfitting them for life's plain work, eating out their love of the Bible, teaching them a false morality, and creating in the soul an unreal standard of truth, and beauty, and love. Don't be too fond of the newspaper. Yet read it, that you may know both what man is doing and what God is doing; and extract out of all you read *matter for thought and prayer*. Avoid works which *jest* with what is right or wrong, lest you unconsciously adopt a false test of truth and duty, namely, ridicule, and so become afraid to do right for right's sake alone; dreading the world's sneer, and undervaluing a good conscience and the approving smile of God. Let your reading be always select; and whatever you read, begin with seeking God's blessing on it. But see that your relish for the Bible be above every other enjoyment, and the moment you begin to feel greater relish for any other book, lay it down till you have sought deliverance from such a snare, and obtained from the Holy Spirit an intenser relish, a keener appetite for the Word of God (*Jer. 15, v. 16*; *Ps. 19, vv. 7-10*).

Chapter 7

Take heed to your steps

Beware, not merely of falling, but of stumbling. 'Walk circumspectly, not as fools, but as wise;' like men in an enemy's country, or like travellers climbing a hill, slippery with ice, and terrible with precipices, where every step may be a fall, and every fall a plunge into a chasm. Beware of little slips, slight inconsistencies, as they are called; they are the beginning of all backsliding, and they are in themselves evil, as well as hateful to God. Keep your garments undefiled (*Rev. 3, v. 4*); beware of small spots as well as larger stains or rents; and the moment you discover any speck, however small, go wash in the fountain, that your 'garments may be always white,' and so pleasing in the eyes of Him, whose you are, and whom you serve. 'Crucify the flesh, with its affections and lusts' (*Gal. 5, v. 24*). 'Mortify your members which are upon the earth' (*Col. 3, v. 5*).

Remember the Lord's words to His Church, 'Thou hast a few names, even in Sardis, which have not defiled their garments, and they shall walk with me in white, for they are worthy.' Stand aloof from the world's gaiety, and be jealous of what are called 'harmless amusements.' I do not condemn *all* amusements, but I ask that they should be *useful and profitable*, not merely harmless. Dancing and card-playing are the world's devices for killing time. They are bits of the world and the world's ways which will ensnare your feet and lead you away from the cross. Let them alone. Keep away from the ball-room, the opera, the oratorio, the theatre. Dress, finery, and display, are deadly snares. Put away levity and frivolity; all silly conversation, or gossip; remembering the apostle's words, 'Neither filthiness, nor *foolish talking, nor jesting*, which are not convenient' (*Eph. 5, v. 4*); and, 'Let no corrupt communication proceed out of your mouth, but that which is good to the use of edifying, that it may minister grace of the hearers; and grieve not the Holy Spirit of God, whereby ye are sealed unto the day of redemption' (*Eph. 4, vv. 29, 30*).

'Flee *youthful* lusts,' if you be young men or women; flee *all* lusts, whether you be young or old. Shun light company, and take no pleasure in the conversation of 'vain persons'. 'Abstain from all appearance of evil.' Be thou a Christian in little things as well as great. Dread little sins, little errors, little omissions of duty. Beware of false steps; and if betrayed into one, retrace it as soon as discovered. If persevered in, the consequences may be months of sorrow.

> That cherished sin, 'twill cost thee dear.

Remember, as a French writer remarks, that, sooner or later, 'every crown of flowers becomes a crown of thorns.'

Redeem the time: much of your progress depends on this. Be men of *method and punctuality*; waste no moments; have always something to do, and *do it*; use up the little spaces of life, the little intervals between engagements. I knew a friend who, one winter, read through some five or six octavo volumes, by making use of the brief interval between family worship and breakfast. Pack up your life well; your trunk will contain twice as much if well packed; attend, then, to the packing of each day and hour. You may save *years* by this. How many have 'slipped' and 'fallen' through idleness! How many *begin* a score of things and end nothing, 'dawdle' away their morning or their evening hours, sleep longer than is needful, trifle through their duties, hurrying about from work to work, or from book to book, or from meeting to meeting, instead of being calm, methodical, energetic! Thus life is loitered away, and each sun sets upon twelve wasted hours, and an uneasy, dissatisfied conscience. Be *punctual and regular* in all duties and engagements. Keep no man waiting. Be honest as to *time*, both with yourselves and others, lest you get into a state of chronic flurry and excitement; so destructive of peace and progress; so grieving to the Spirit, whose very nature is calmness and rest.

These may seem small things, but they are the roots of great. Resist beginnings. 'Seize time by the fore-lock.' Live while you live. Watch your steps; count your minutes; live as men who are pressing on to a kingdom, and who fear, not only open apostasy, but the smallest measure of coming short, the slightest stain upon the garment of a saint, the faintest slur upon the name of a disciple (*Heb. 4, v. 1*; *Jude v. 23*).

Watch against special sins; or things that have 'the appearance of evil;' or things that lead into evil, and discredit 'that worthy name by which you are called' (*1 Thess. 5, v. 22*; *Jas. 2, v. 7*). If you have a bad temper, watch against that. If you have a rude way of speech, a cold, distant, repulsive manner, or are ill to please, look well to these, and 'be courteous' (*1 Pet. 3, v. 8*). If you are covetous in disposition, or shabby in your dwellings, or niggardly in your givings, take care; 'the love of money is the root of all evil.' If you are slovenly in your dress, or untidy in your person, or unpolite in your demeanour, set yourself to rectify these blemishes. If you are lazy, luxurious, given to the good things of this life, or selfish, disobliging, unneighbourly, rude, blunt, unbrotherly, look to your Pattern, and see if these things were in Him. If you are fickle, and frivolous, and flippant, greedy of jokes, carried away with immoderate laughter, be upon your guard. If you are romantic and sentimental, take care lest the indulgence of such a temperament should land you in peevishness, self-pity, and a cowardly avoidance of the common duties of life. If you are censorious, captious, fault-finding, proud, domineering, supercilious, and sulky, get the unclean spirit cast out forthwith. If you be a gossip, or a gadabout, or a busy-body in other men's matters, take care, for at such crevices Satan creeps in. If you be secretive and cunning, with a certain littleness or slyness in your nature, which never lets you forget your own interests, beware! Christ was not such; Paul was not such. Be frank, open, manly. Remember the summing-up of David's picture of the blessed man, 'in whose spirit there is *no guile*' (*Ps. 32, v. 2*). Be not 'Jacob,' a man of guile; but *Israel*, a noble prince — 'an *Israelite* indeed, in whom is no guile' (*John 1, v. 48*).

Walk 'straight up,' along the path of life, like a forgiven man, with God at your side (*Gen. 5, v. 24, 6, v. 9*), and with the joy of the Lord for your strength

(*Neh. 8, v. 9; Eccles. 9, v. 7*); doing heartily your daily work, whether sacred or common, with an unshaded brow and an earnest but cheerful face. In short, watch against your *old self* at every point.

Do not evade these remarks by saying that some of the things spoken of are trifles, and beneath notice. Nothing should be too small for a Christian to notice, either of right or wrong. Remember the Master's words about denying *self* — every part of self; be not a servant of self, or a worshipper of self, or a 'lover of self' (*2 Tim. 3, v. 1*) in any form. Take up your cross, and follow your Lord (*Matt. 16, v. 24*); as it is written, 'Even Christ pleased not Himself' (*Rom. 15, v. 3*).

Chapter 8

Put away boastfulness and love of praise

God's aim in all His doings of grace is to 'hide pride from man;' to hinder boasting; to keep the sinner humble. All that the old Christian can say is, 'By the grace of God I am what I am;' and the youngest has no other confidence or boast. All 'confidence in the flesh' (*Phil. 3, v. 1*), all trust in self, all reliance on the creature, are set aside by that great work of the Divine Substitute, who did all for us, and left us nothing to do, out of which it would be possible to extract a boast (*2 Cor. 12, v. 9; Gal. 6, v. 14; Isa. 41, v. 16, 45, v. 25*).

The sinner's first act of believing is his consenting to be treated as a sinner, and simply as such; indebted for nothing to himself, in any shape or in any sense, but wholly to God and to His free love, in Christ Jesus our Lord. This was the laying down of all pride and boastfulness. Then he knew the meaning of the words, 'Glory ye in His holy *name*' (1 Chron. 16, v. 10); for *the name* in which he then began to glory was the name revealed in Exodus (*Ex. 34, v. 6*); the *name* that assured him of the love of that God with whom he had to do.

Self was set aside, and Christ came in, *to do and to be all that self had hitherto been supposed to be and to do*. What things before were gain to us, these we then counted loss for Christ; and we ceased for ever to glory in the flesh, or to be debtors to anything but the blood and righteousness of the Son of God. We learned to say, 'God forbid that we should glory, save in the cross of our Lord Jesus Christ' (*Gal. 6, v. 14*).

We ceased to work for salvation, for we had got it without working; and we had got it, not in order that we might indulge in sin because grace abounded, but in order that, having our legal bonds all loosed and our prison opened, we might henceforth serve God with our whole heart and soul. We thus became debtors, 'not to the *flesh*, to live after the flesh' (*Rom. 8, v. 12*); — for the flesh had done nothing for us, and we owed it nothing; — but debtors to God and to His love: not to *self* or the old man, for these had brought us only sin and evil; but to Jesus Christ and His precious blood: not to *law*, for it only condemned us, and held us in bondage; but to that 'free Spirit' (*Ps. 51, v. 12*), that 'good Spirit' (*Neh. 9, v. 20*), that 'Spirit of life which makes us free from the law of sin and death' (*Rom. 8, v. 2*). Thus everything that could cause pride was swept away at the outset; and that not by law, but by the very necessity of the case, by the very nature of that salvation which was brought to us; not through anything which we either could or could not do, but *through the love, and work, and blood of another*.

Let us fling away self-esteem and high-mindedness, for it is the very essence of unbelief, as the prophet told Israel, 'Hear ye, and give ear; be not *proud*, for the Lord hath spoken' (*Jer. 13, v. 15*). Be meek, be poor in spirit, be humble; be teachable, be gentle, and easy to be entreated; putting away all high thoughts and lofty imaginations, either about what we are or what we can do; content to take the obscurest corner and the lowest seat; and this, not to indulge in a false lowliness, or in 'the pride that apes humility,' feeding our vanity with the thought that we are martyrs, and puffing up our fleshly mind with the idea of our wonderful condescension, or by brooding over our supposed wrongs and trials. Let us be *truly* humble, as was the Son of God: content to live unknown, and to do our work unnoticed, as a work not for the eye of man, but of God.

Put away all envy, and jealousy of others, as well as all malice and evil-speaking (*Eph. 4, v. 31*). Love to hear of a brother's prosperity. Don't grudge him a few words of honest praise; nor try maliciously to turn the edge of it, by an envious 'but,' or a grave silence, or a wise shake of the head; unless you have very special reasons for disallowing the eulogy. Remember that Solomon's 'wicked man' is one that 'winketh with his eyes, and speaketh with his feet, and teacheth with his fingers' (*Prov. 6, v. 13, 10, v. 10*). Have a care of detraction and backbiting; speak of a person's faults only to himself and to God. Be not censorious or uncharitable, in thought or word. *Inconsistent Christians are often more censorious than the world*; for they need to apologize to themselves for their inconsistencies by detracting from the excellencies of those who are more consistent than themselves, and by trying to believe that good men are no better than others.

Some love to *speak*; and show their pride in this way, both in private and in public. If you are young, and newly led out of your former ignorance, beware of this snare. Remember Paul's advice — 'Not a *novice* (that is, one newly converted), lest being lifted up with pride, he fall into condemnation and the snare of the devil' (*1 Tim. 3, v. 6*). If you have gifts, use them quietly and modestly, not ostentatiously. Do not be forward to tell your experience, or give your opinion, or to take rank above your seniors. Do not think that all zeal or wisdom is confined to you and a few about you. Do not condemn others because they don't go quite along with you in all things; nor speak of them as cold, and dead, and unspiritual. Do not think that no one cares for souls but yourselves; that no one can state the gospel or pray like you; or that God is not likely to bless any one so much as you. Be lowly; and show this, not by always speaking evil of yourselves to others, or by using the conceited phrase 'in my humble opinion' (as some do in order to show their humility), but by not speaking of yourselves at all. Keep *self* in the background, and don't say or do anything that looks like baiting your hook for a little praise.

Some love to *rule and manage*. So did Diotrephes (*3 John, v. 9*). They are not happy, unless they are at the head of everything — the originators of all plans, the presidents of societies, the speakers at meetings. Beware of this love of pre-eminence, as ruinous to your own soul and injurious to the Church of God. If God puts work into your hands, do it; and do it faithfully, through good report or bad report. Bear to be contradicted and spoken against. Do not fret when things go wrong with you or your schemes; nor get 'petted' like a spoilt child when you don't get your own way; nor fling up everything in disgust when you happen to be thwarted. Do not take yourself for Solomon, or suppose that wisdom will die with you (*Job 12, v. 2*). If called to preside or manage, do it; and do it with energy and authority, as one who has a trust to fulfil. But 'mind not high things' (*Rom. 12, v. 16*); 'Seek not great things for thyself' (*Jer. 45, v. 5*); 'He that is greatest among you, let him be as the younger; and he that is chief, as he that doth serve' (*Luke 22, v. 26*); 'All of you be subject one to another' (*1 Pet. 5, v. 5*); 'In honour preferring one another' (*Rom. 12, v. 10*).

Yet be *discriminating*. Do not call error truth for the sake of charity. Do not praise earnest men merely because they are earnest. To be earnest in truth is one thing; to be earnest in error is another. The first is blessed, not so much because of the earnestness, but because of the truth; the second is hateful to God, and ought to be shunned by you. Remember how the Lord Jesus, from heaven, spoke concerning *error*: 'which thing I *hate*' (*Rev. 2, vv. 6-15; 1 Tim. 6, vv. 4, 5*). True *spiritual discernment* is much lost sight of as a real Christian grace; discernment between the evil and the good, the false and the true. 'Beloved, believe not every spirit; but try the spirits whether they are of God; because many false prophets are gone out into the world' (*1 John 4, v. 1*). This 'discernment', which belongs to every one who is taught of God, is the very opposite of that which is called in our day by the boastful name of 'liberality.' Spiritual discernment and 'liberal thought' have little in common with each other. 'Abhor that which is evil, cleave to that which is good' (*Rom. 12, v. 9*). The 'liberality which puts bitter for sweet, and sweet for bitter' (*Isa. 5, v. 20*), is a very different thing from the 'charity which thinketh no evil' (*1 Cor. 13, v. 5*). Truth is a mighty thing in the eyes of God, whatever it may be in those of men. All error is, more or less, whether directly or indirectly, a misrepresentation of God's character, and a subversion of His revelation (*Rev. 22, vv. 18, 19*).

Chapter 9

Watch against Satan

He is above all others your enemy; he, the 'old serpent,' the 'dragon,' the 'liar and murderer' from the beginning. It is with him that you are to fight. 'For we wrestle not against flesh and blood (that is, earthly foes, men like ourselves), but against principalities, against powers, against the rulers of the darkness of this world, against spiritual wickedness in high places' (*Eph. 6, v. 12*). The world tries to bewitch and beguile us; but it is the 'god of this world,' the 'prince of this world,' the 'prince of the power of the air,' that so especially lays snares for us, making use of the world's beauty, and pleasure, and vanity for leading us captive at his will. 'O how (as one has written) are thou intrenched, O Satan — how art thou intrenched in thy beautiful deceptions; thou hast played thy part well in these last days; thou art all but the Holy One, thou consummate deceiver!' It is this that gives to the ball-room, and the dance, and the theatre, and the voluptuous music their special power to harm; for these are Satan's baits and nets, by means of which he allures the unwary, and leads back the believer to unbelieving ground, disarming our watchfulness, dazzling our vision, reviving our worldliness, and perhaps, for a season, lulling us wholly asleep. We know that through his successful wiles, perilous times are to come, when many, while lovers of self, traitors, heady, high-minded, lovers of pleasure, are still to have the 'form of godliness' (*2 Tim. 3, vv. 1-4*); and we know that the last days are to be like the days of Noah and Lot (*Luke 17, vv. 26-32*), days of revelling, and banqueting, and luxury. Let us be wary, lest, standing as we do on the edge of these days, we be drawn away into the sins of an age led captive by Satan at his will.

Resist the devil, and he will flee from you. Fight the good fight of faith against him and his hosts. Watch unto prayer. 'Be sober, be vigilant; because your adversary, the devil, as a roaring lion, walketh about, seeking whom he may devour' (*1 Pet. 5, v. 8*). In these last days he will lay his snares more cunningly than ever, to deceive, if it were possible, the very elect. He is coming down, having great wrath, because he knoweth he hath but a short time (*Rev. 12, v. 12*).

Chapter 10

Beware of one-sided truth

There are few things more dangerous or more likely to lead into open error. Take care, for instance, of misunderstanding what the Scripture says about the old man and the new man, the flesh and the spirit, and so making void your own personal responsibility for all you say and do, and also setting aside the necessity for the blood of Christ, as daily needed for our whole person, and the power of the Spirit, as needed constantly for our whole being, as long as we live.

Our Lord and His apostles use many figures to show the greatness of the change produced by being begotten again. They speak of this change as being an actual indwelling of Christ Himself personally. 'Christ in you, the hope of glory' (*Col. 1, v. 27*); 'Christ liveth in me' (*Gal. 2, v. 20*); that 'Christ may dwell in your hearts by faith' (*Eph. 3, v. 17*). But this living and indwelling of Christ does not make us the same as Christ, or Christ the same as we; nor does it make the blood and the Spirit less necessary. It does not make Christ responsible for our sins, nor does it make us sinless. It does not lead us to say, You need not care what you do, for Christ dwells in you, and all you do is His doing.

Again, on the other hand, Scripture speaks of our 'being in Christ' (*2 Cor. 5, v.17; 1 Cor. 1, v. 30*). But our being in Christ does not mean that we (that is, our whole man, body, soul, and spirit) are actually put into Christ as water is put into a vessel. This would destroy the sense; and besides, it would either make us sinless, or it would make Christ the author of our sins, and the doer of all that we do. These figures do mean that there is such a wonderful nearness between Christ and us, such a living connection, that we receive His power and fulness; but they do not mean that we and Christ are no longer two persons, but one, — no longer two bodies, but one — no longer two souls, but one.

Again, in the Old Testament the Holy Spirit says, 'A new heart also will I give you, and a new spirit will I put within you; and I will take away the stony heart out of your flesh, and I will give you a heart of flesh' (*Ezek. 36, v. 26*). This does not mean that an actual *stone*, whether of granite or marble, is taken out of us, and an actual piece of flesh (created in heaven) is inserted instead. Nor does it mean that *the whole* of our old nature is at once taken out of us, leaving no part behind, and that a complete new nature is substituted, so that there shall be absolutely nothing in us but what is perfect and divine. If this be the meaning of the figure, then every conversion must be the passing into instantaneous perfection, no fragment of the old nature being left behind, and no feature of the new nature being left unperfected or undeveloped. Thus there could be no conflict, no difficulty, no declension, *no possibility of backsliding*. The change thus figured to us is certainly a very great one, but it cannot mean the changing of one person into another, nor the transformation of a man into an angel.

Again, our Lord says to Nicodemus, 'Except a man

be *born again*, he cannot see the kingdom of God' (*John 3, v. 3*). Nicodemus took Him literally, and so destroyed the whole meaning of this divine symbol. Those in our day who maintain that actually and literally a new created thing is dropped into us at conversion, which they call the new man, are saying exactly what Nicodemus said, 'Can a man enter the second time into his mother's womb and be born?' The new birth does not mean a new *person*. Christ did not mean that Nicodemus was no longer to be Nicodemus, or that Peter was no longer to be Peter, after conversion; but that such a spiritual work was to take place as to change their whole spiritual nature and character, while leaving them still Nicodemus and Peter, with all their original and proper personalities and humanities. Our Lord does not say, Except *a part of a man* is born again; but, Except *a man* is born again. The change may not be perfect at first, but it affects the *whole* man: so that he cannot say of himself, A part of me is born again, and a part of me is not born again; but, *I* am born again.

Connected with this there are the statements regarding the new creature: 'If any man be in Christ, he is a new creature' (or, 'there is a new creation'): 'old things are passed away; behold, all things are become new' (*2 Cor. 5, v. 17*). It is not that a new creature has been put into a man, like new wine into old vessels; but *the whole man is the new creature*, and is regarded as such by God from the day of his being born again. That the transformation is perfect and complete *from the outset*, the figure does not imply; that it will one day be all that is thus symbolized, it assures us beyond a doubt. So with regard to the flesh and the spirit, the old man and the new. The flesh is the man (call him Peter or Paul), with the remnants of his former self about him; the *spirit* is the same man (it may be Peter or Paul), with the new life unfolding itself within him. The *figure* names *two* men, the old and the new; but we are not, like Nicodemus, to take the words in a carnal or ultra-literal sense; for, after all, *the man* is but one all the while.

For thus the apostle speaks: '*I* am dead to the law, that I might live unto God. *I* am crucified with Christ: nevertheless *I* live; yet not *I* but Christ liveth in me' (*Gal. 2, vv. 19, 20*). He does not say here, My *old man* is dead, but, I myself am dead; not, My old man is crucified, but, I myself am crucified; and this same person (I myself) who is dead and crucified *still liveth*. He does not say, One section of me is dead, and another is living; but, I myself am dead, and I myself am living: I, the same person, am both a dead and a living man. This is the real sense of the figure.

This conflict, not between two *persons*, but between two parts (or conditions) of one person, is that which the apostle brings out in the 7th of the Romans: 'I was alive. . . . I died. . . . I am carnal, sold under sin. . . . That which I do I allow not: . . . what I would, that do I not; . . . what I hate, that do I. . . . In me (that is, in my flesh) dwelleth no good thing: . . . to will is present with me; how to perform I find not. . . . The good that I would I do not: the evil which I would not, that I do. . . . It is no more I that do it, but sin that dwelleth in me. . . . When I would do good, evil is present with me. . . . I delight in the law of God after the inward man: but I see another law in my members. . . . Who shall deliver me from the body of this death?' It is Paul himself, speaking for himself, speaking as one delighting in the law of God, that utters these strange things, these seeming contradictions. It is not a perfect part of Paul fighting against an imperfect part of Paul; but it is Paul himself fighting against Paul himself. The one Paul, the one person, has two conflicting elements within him, each striving for the mastery. 'The inward man,' says he, 'is renewed day by day' (*2 Cor. 4, v. 16*). This process of daily renewal is that which goes on within him. The light and the darkness struggle together, but the light conquers, and shines more and more unto the perfect day.

Beware specially of this onesidedness in everything connected with Christ Himself. Faith connects us with the Person of Christ in all its parts and aspects. It connects us with *the whole work of Christ* from the cradle to the throne, from Bethlehem to the heaven of heavens. It connects us with His birth, His life, His death, His burial, His resurrection, His ascension and glory. Out of all these it draws life and strength. Life in a crucified Christ, life in a risen Christ, life in a glorified Christ, — this is the heritage of faith. Out of death, the death of that cross where He was crucified through weakness, come life and power to us; and down from the throne on which He now sits, the possessor and dispenser of that Spirit of promise, these same blessings come. In the cross is power. In the resurrection is power. In the throne of that glory there is power. It is as the *glorified* Christ (*John 7, v. 39*) that He has received for us the Spirit with all His gifts (*Ps. 68, v. 18*; *Eph. 4, vv. 7-13*). It is with the *glorified* Christ that we are linked by faith, for blessing, for power, for life, for consolation. 'Because I live, ye shall live also.'

Chapter 11

Do something for God

You were neither born nor re-born for yourselves alone. You may not be able to do much, but do something; work while it is day. You may not be able to give much, but give something; according to your ability, remembering that the Lord loveth a cheerful giver. Take heed, and beware of covetousness; for the love of money is the root of all evil. Whenever worldliness comes in, in any shape, whether it be love of money or love of pleasure, you cease to be faithful to Christ, and are trying to serve both God and mammon.

Do something, then, for God, while time lasts. It may not be long; for the day goeth away, and the shadows of evening are stretched out. Do something every day. Work, and throw your heart into the work. Work joyfully and with a right good will, as men who love both their work and their master. Be not weary in well-doing. Work, and work in faith. Work in love, and patience, and hope. Don't shrink from hard labour or disagreeable duties, or a post trying to flesh and blood. 'Endure hardness, as a good soldier in Jesus Christ' (*2 Tim. 2, v. 3*). Be stedfast, unmoveable, always abounding in the work of the Lord (*1 Cor. 15, v. 58*). Don't fold your hands, or lay aside your staff, or sheathe your sword. Don't give way to slothfulness and flesh-pleasing; saying to yourselves, 'I can get to heaven without working.'

Your gifts may be small, your time not much, your opportunities few; but work, and do it quietly, without bustle, or self-importance, not as pleasing men, but God; not seeking the honour that cometh from men, but that which cometh from God. The day of honour is coming, and the Master's 'Well done' will make up for all hardship and labour here. When the Son of man shall come in His glory, with all His holy angels, and when He shall sit upon the throne of His glory, it will be blessed to be set upon His right hand, and acknowledged as those who have fed Him, and clothed and visited Him in prison; and it would be a bitter thing, indeed, to be 'saved so as by fire,' namely: barely saved, and no more; saved (if such a thing can be thought of) without doing anything for Him that saved us; having given Him no water when He was thirsty, no food when He was hungry, no clothes when He was naked, and when in prison having never once come nigh Him.

Chapter 12

Live waiting for your Lord

He that loves Christ will long to see Him, and will not be content with the interviews which faith gives. The lover seeks the absent loved one; the wife the husband; the child the mother: so do you your Lord. It is not enough that you can communicate with Him daily by the epistles which faith brings and carries; you must see Him face to face, otherwise there is a blank in your life, a void in your existence, a cloud over your love, and a faltering in your song. The saved one desires to meet his Saviour, and feels that his joy must be imperfect till then. It is the mark of a disciple that he 'waits for the Son of God from heaven' (*1 Thess. 1, v. 10*); that he loves, looks for, longs for the appearance of Christ. Let this mark be seen on you; and be like the Corinthian saints, of whom it was told by their apostle, 'Ye come behind in no gift, waiting for the coming of our Lord Jesus Christ' (*1 Cor. 1, v. 7*). 'Gird up the loins of your mind, be sober, and hope to the end for the grace that is to be brought unto you at the revelation of Jesus Christ' (*1 Pet. 1, v. 13*).

Chapter 13

The Lord our God

'I am the Lord your God,' was God's greeting of love to Israel (*Lev. 11, v. 44*): it is no less now His salutation of grace to every one who has believed on the name of His Son, Christ Jesus. God becomes our God the moment that we receive His testimony to His beloved Son. This new relationship between God and us, in virtue of which He calls us *His*, and we call Him ours, is the simple result of a believed gospel.

If any one reading these lines is led to ask, How may I become a son? we answer in the words of truth, 'He that believeth that Jesus is the Christ, is born of God.' Nothing less than believing can bring about this sonship; and nothing more is needed. The joy, and the peace, and the love, and the warmth, these are the *effects* of faith, but they are not faith; they are the fruits of a conscious sonship which has been formed by the belief of the divine testimony to Jesus as the Son of God and the Saviour of the lost. 'As many as received Him, to them gave He the right of being sons of God, even to them that believed on His name' (*John 1, v. 12*). God's simple message of grace contains peace for the sinner; and the sinner extracts the peace therein contained, not by effort or feeling, but by the simple belief of the true sayings of God. Good news make glad by being believed, and they refuse to yield up their precious treasure to anything but to simple faith. Believe the tidings of peace from God, and the peace is all your own.

It is not to him that worketh, or feeleth, or loveth, but to him that believeth that God says, 'I am the Lord your God.' And when God used the word *believing*, He just meant what He said, and intended nothing else than what man means by that word. Had He meant anything else, He would have told us, and not suffered us to be misled or deceived by our misunderstanding of a word of which the Bible is full. Had He meant working, or feeling, or loving, He would have said so, and not allowed us to suppose that believing was really all. What a book of deception and mystery the Bible would be, if 'believing' does not mean 'believing', but something less or something more! To make it something less, would be to take from God's word as truly as if we had struck out a book from the Bible. To make it something more, would be to add to God's word, as truly and as sinfully as if we had forged another Gospel or another Epistle, or accepted the Apocrypha as part of the inspired record. We make God a liar when we refuse to take Him at His word, or give Him credit for speaking that simple truth, in believing which we are saved; but let us remember the other side of his statement, namely, our being found liars by reason of our adding to His word. 'Every word of God is pure' (*Prov. 30, v. 5*); can we make it purer, or more transparent, or more simple? We add to it, lest it should be too simple, too childlike, too blessed; we put something of our own into it to make it more 'substantial' and complete; and that something (call it feeling, or realizing, or loving) destroys the divine simplicity and transparency of faith. 'Add thou not unto His words, lest He reprove thee, and thou be found a liar' (*Prov. 30, v. 6*). Does casting dust upon the sunbeam improve its quality or make it more like the sun from which it came? Would pouring filth into a cup of pure spring water make it more lucid and refreshing? Whatever we add to *believing*, tends to destroy its real nature and to mar its effects. If God had said that we are to be saved by believing that the deluge overflowed the earth, and that the sun once stood still in the heavens, we should have understood what He meant by the word. And is there any more difficulty in understanding Him when He says, 'He that *believeth* is justified from all things'? Does believing mean one thing in Genesis and another in Romans? Does it mean one thing to Abraham and another to us? Does it mean one thing today and another tomorrow? Or is not the formula of salvation, 'Believe in the Lord Jesus Christ, and thou shalt be saved,' meant to be the simplest and most intelligible of all declarations ever made to man?

We believe the Holy Spirit's testimony, that Jesus died and rose again, 'the Just for the unjust.' That saves. We believe the divine promise annexed to this testimony, that life is the possession of every man who believeth this heavenly testimony; and this *belief of the promise* (which some call appropriation) *assures* us, on God's word, that life is ours personally. We do not *get* life by believing that life is ours; nor do we get Christ by believing that Christ is ours. This is as absurd as the idea of getting our debts paid by believing that they are paid. But we get life and Christ by believing God's glad tidings concerning Jesus and His finished work upon the cross. There is enough in Christ to pay every man's debt; but no man's debt is actually paid until he has taken God at His word, and believed the record which God has given of His Son.

It is the blood that pacifies my conscience. The sight of it is all I need to remove fear and impart confidence. It is not my 'seeing that I see it' that gives me boldness, but my direct and simple sight of it. My guilt passes away from me so soon as I believe; and I don't need to wait *till I believe in my own act of believing* before becoming conscious of this deliverance. The blood contains my pardon and my peace; and by looking at it I extract the pardon and the peace. I don't need to look at my looking; I need only to look at the blood. If I cannot extract from it pardon and peace, I never shall be able to extract them from my own act of seeing. I am to believe in Jesus; not in my own faith, nor in my own feelings. I am to look to the cross, not to my own convictions or repentance. The well of peace is not within me; and to let down my bucket into my own heart for the purpose of drawing up the water of peace, is mockery as well as foolishness. I do not fill the cup of peace out of anything that is in myself. Christ has filled that cup already, — long, long ago; — and in love He presses it to my parched lips. Let me drink at once of it, for all the peace of God, the peace of heaven is there.

When God said to Israel, 'I am the Lord your God,' He added this, 'Ye shall therefore *sanctify* yourselves; and ye shall be *holy*, for I am holy' (*Lev. 11, v. 44*); and He added this also, 'I am the Lord that bringeth you up out of the land of Egypt to be your God: ye shall therefore be *holy*, for I am holy' (*ib. 45*).

God calls us to be *holy*. He becomes our God to make us *like Himself*. 'He calls us to be partakers of the divine nature, having escaped the corruption that is in the world through lust.' He expects that we should represent Him among our fellow-men by our resemblance to Himself.

The carrying out of this holiness is His own work, — the operation of His Spirit. Whether our perfection in holiness is to be wrought gradually or instantaneously, is a question to be determined solely by His word, and not by any theories of our own. That God *could* make each soul perfect the moment he believes, we admit; — that He may have wise reasons for not doing this, — wise reasons for *gradual growth*, — will not be denied. He has given us no instance in the Bible of any one made instantaneously sinless, either at his conversion or during his after life. All the men of faith and holiness, the men 'full of the Holy Ghost,' which He presents to us as our models, are imperfect men to the end of their days, needing forgiveness and cleansing constantly. He glorifies Himself in our imperfect bodies; in an imperfect Church, on an imperfect earth. His object here is to glorify Himself in *imperfection and growth*, as He is hereafter to glorify Himself in perfection and completeness of every kind. Gradual growth is the law of all things here, — man, beasts, trees, and flowers, — so that unless we had some very notable example in Scripture of a sinless man, or of miraculous and instantaneous perfection by an act of faith, we are not disposed to accept the theory of instantaneous sinlessness, as that to which we are called in believing; even though that be veiled under the specious name of 'entire consecration,' or accompanied with the profession of personal unworthiness, — a 'personal unworthiness' which, however, does not seem to require any actual confession of sin.

Yet God calls us to be holy. He expects us to grow in *unlikeness* to this world, and in *likeness* to that world which is to come. He expects us to follow Him who did no sin, even though the attainment of perfection should not be in a day or a year, but the growth of a lifetime. It is for want of daily *growth*, not for want of complete and constant sinlessness, that God so often challenges His own.

Let us *grow*. Let us bring forth fruit. 'Put ye on the Lord Jesus Christ, and make not provision for the flesh to fulfil the lusts thereof.' What is the use of taking so long to make us sinless? — some may say. I answer, Go and ask God. What was the use of taking six days to bring creation to perfection? Why did He let sin enter our world when He could have kept it out? What was the use of not making the whole Church perfect at once? Why did He not make Abraham or David or Paul perfect at once? He could have done so. Why did He not?

Let us study soberly and truly the word of God in regard to *the past history of His saints*, lest it be said to some in our day who think themselves on a far 'higher platform' than others, — more perfect than Paul or John, — 'Nay but, O man, who art thou that repliest against God? shall the thing formed say to Him that formed it, Why hast Thou made me thus?'

Let us grow. The impatience that demands instantaneous perfection is *unbelief, refusing to recognise God's spiritual laws in the new creation*. The gradual evolution of the heavenly life in a lifelong course of conflict and imperfection, is the way in which sin is unfolded, the human heart exposed to view, the power of the cross tested, the efficacy of the blood manifested, and the power as well as the love of Father, Son, and Spirit magnified. God's purpose is not simply to reveal Himself, but to reveal man, — not simply man dead in trespasses and sin, but man after he has been made alive unto righteousness, to exhibit, step by step, and day by day, that most solemn and humbling of all processes, namely, that by which 'the inward man is renewed day by day' (*2 Cor. 4, v. 16*): while the strength of the human will for evil is manifested, the awful tenacity of sin shown forth, and the absolute hopelessness of any sinner's salvation demonstrated, save by the omnipotence of God Himself.

Let us grow daily and hourly. Let us grow down; let us grow up. Let us strike our roots deeper; let us spread out our branches more widely. Let us not only 'blossom and bud,' but let us bring forth fruit, ripe and plentiful, on every bough. 'Herein is my Father glorified, that ye bear much fruit; so shall ye be my disciples' (*John 15, v. 8*).

Chapter 14

Hindrances to avoid

Many things can hinder growth and fruit-bearing. Mark the following:

Unbelief

'So we see they could not enter in because of unbelief' (*Heb. 3, v. 19*). This poisons the tree at its very root. Christ can do no mighty works in us, or for us, because of unbelief (*Matt. 13, v. 58*). 'Only believe' (*Mark 5, v. 36*). 'Have faith in God' (*Mark 11, v. 22*). 'He that believeth' (*Mark 9, v. 23*). 'He that believeth on me, out of his belly shall flow rivers of living water' (*John 7, v. 38*).

Want of love

No love, no fruit; much love, much fruit (*Heb. 10, v. 24*). 'Labour of love' means the labour which love produces, to which love stimulates (*1 Thess. 1, v. 3*). Love is by its very nature *fruit-bearing*. When 'love waxes cold' (*Matt. 24, v. 12*), — when we 'leave our first love' (*Rev. 2, v. 4*), then everything that deserves the name of fruit dies away. If there be fruit at all, it is poor and unripe. Our zeal is the zeal of Jehu (*2 Kings 10, v. 16*); our warmth is false fire; our energy is the vigour of the flesh; our work is the work of men urged on by a false stimulus; our words, however earnest, are the words of *excited self*. If any one ask, How am I to get love? I answer, Look to Jesus, deal with Him about it, learn anew to love by learning anew His love to you. I do not say 'Work, and that will stimulate you to love.' No. It is not first work, and then love; but first love, and then work. Get more love by dealing more with Jesus personally, and then love will set you all on fire. You will work unbidden; you will work in the liberty of fellowship and in the joy of love (*1 Thess. 3, v. 12; Gal. 5, v. 6; 2 Cor. 5, v. 14*).

Selfishness (*Mark 8, v. 34*)

Self in all its forms is a hindrance to our growth (*Rom. 14, v. 7*). Self-will, self-sufficiency, self-indulgence, self-importance, self-glory, self-seeking, self-brooding, — all these mar fruitfulness. Denying self is the beginning, the middle, and the end of our course here, as followers of Christ. Selfishness takes the form of covetousness, or love of money; of luxury, or love of meats and drinks, and the good things of this life; of religious dissipation, or love of excitement; of spiritual restlessness, or running from meeting to meeting, or book to book, or opinion to opinion, or minister to minister; of craving for religious stimulants and spices, with loathing of what is tame or common, however good and true. These are some of the forms of selfishness which destroy both growth and fruitfulness. How can a man *grow* when he is pampering self instead of crucifying the flesh; when he is indulging and fondling the old man instead of nailing him to the cross; when he is enjoying all softness and ease and worldly comfort, instead of enduring hardness, and taking up his cross and mortifying his members which are upon the earth? (*Rom. 8, v. 13; Gal. 5, v. 24; Col. 3, v. 5*).

Covetousness

'The love of money is the root of all evil' (*1 Tim. 6, v. 10*). Few things are more hateful in a Christian man than this; few things more completely destroy his influence; and few things more sadly or more justly make him the scorn of the world than eagerness for money, or niggardliness in parting with it. The covetous man cannot grow. He must ever remain a stunted Christian. 'Filthy lucre' is poison to the soul. If we do not 'make friends of the mammon of unrighteousness' by laying out our substance for God, it will become the blight of spirituality, the destruction of our religious life (*Prov. 30, v. 8; 1 Tim. 6, vv. 6-10*). Be generous, be large-hearted, be open-handed, be loving, be free in giving, if you would grow.

Pride

Self-satisfaction in any shape, or self-admiration of any kind, in regard to person, or property, or accomplishments, or position; these are immensely hurtful to spiritual life. True godliness prospers only in the lowly heart; the heart which, in proportion as it becomes more and more satisfied with Christ, becomes more and more dissatisfied with itself. If the Master was meek and lowly, shall the disciple be anything else?

Easy-mindedness

To take things easy is by some reckoned a great virtue; and not to get warm or excited or zealous, is regarded as proof of a noble and well-balanced mind. We might admit this to be the case, were it confined to worldly matters. To lose a fortune, and yet be calm, is well. To endure provocation and be unruffled is also well. But to take religion easy is not so to be commended. Easy-going religionists are strangers to the fervour of John or Paul. To be contented while uncertain of our salvation is something very awful. To be contented while making no progress, or perhaps going back, is nearly as awful. Easy-minded religion is just the same as lifeless coldness, though perhaps not so repulsive to others. The good-natured formality of thousands is just the hateful lukewarmness of Laodicea.

But let these hints suffice. They will help a little, and guide a little, and teach a little, and warn a little. In reading them, let there be much self-questioning and self-applying. 'Is it I, Lord, is it I?'

Chapter 15

Be of good cheer

A revival time is one of blessing, but it is one of peril. The running well and the going back, the flocking to the cross and the turning away from it, the warm confession and the subsequent silence, — these are things which have been witnessed in other times, and may be witnessed again. Hence our anxiety to give all the guidance and the counsel that we can. Let the young listen. Let them humble themselves to Christian counsel. Let them take heed and watch narrowly their own footsteps.

But still we would not dishearten any. Be not discouraged, we say; but be of good cheer. Faint not, though you may often be weary. Though we bid you count the cost, yet we say to you, as God said to Israel, 'Behold, the Lord your God hath set the land before thee: go up and possess it, as the Lord God of thy fathers hath said unto thee; *fear not, neither be discouraged*' (*Deut. 1, v. 21*). We would not be of those to whom God spoke, and said, 'Why *discourage* ye the hearts of the people?' (*Num. 32, v. 7*). We remember it is said that 'the soul of the people was much discouraged because of the way' (*Num. 21, v. 4*); and that this *discouragement led to sin*. We would not discourage the weakest; for we call to mind Him who 'breaks not the bruised reed, nor quenches the smoking flax' (*Isa.

42, v. 3); who 'gathers the lambs with His arm, who carries them in His bosom, and who gently leads those that are with young' (*Isa. 40, v. 11*). We say to 'those who are of a fearful heart, Be strong, fear not' (*Isa. 35, v. 4*); and we would 'strengthen the weak hands, and confirm the feeble knees' (*Isa. 35, v. 3*). You say the 'fearful' are among those who are cast into the lake of fire, and you fear you are one of them. Not so. The 'fearful' specified in the Book of Revelation (*chap. 21, v. 28*), are the *cowards* who have refused to confess to Christ, who have turned their back on Christ; and they are very different from the 'fearful' spoken of in Isaiah.

Be of good courage. You have God upon your side. You have Christ to fight for you. You have the Holy Spirit to sustain and comfort you. You have more encouragements than discouragements. You have the example of millions that have gone before you. You have exceeding great and precious promises (*2 Pet. 1, v. 4*). You have many fellow-travellers and fellow-soldiers on the right hand and on the left. You have a bright kingdom in view which will compensate for all trial and conflict here. And then, the way is short. The toil will soon be over. The battle will not last for ever. Greater is He that is with you than all that can be against you. Be strong in the Lord. Be strong in His love and in His power. Take to you the whole armour of God (*Eph. 6, vv. 10, 11*).

Do you say that you are in Christ, and that you are abiding in Him? Then you *ought* to walk as He walked. You are *bound* to follow His footsteps; and if you say that you are *not bound* to do so, you set aside the divine teaching of the apostle here given us.

The man who says, 'I am Christ's,' is *under obliga-*

tions to imitate Him. Duty and love alike constrain him to do so; not duty without love, nor yet love without duty. Duty without love would mean reluctance and compulsion; love without duty would mean love fixed upon an unlawful object, whom it was not right to love. Duty and love going together mean that our love is fixed upon a worthy and lawful object; in loving whom we are *feeling* what is right, and in obeying whom we are *doing* what is right.

If I love that which it is not my duty to love, I sin. If I love that which it is my duty to love, I am doing the right thing, — the thing which God delights in. If I honour my parents, I do so for two reasons: (1) Because God has said, Honour thy father and thy mother; (2) Because I love them. The two things, the duty and the love, are in perfect harmony with each other. It is a dutiful thing to love, and it is a loving thing to be dutiful.

Suppose you have a mother in Scotland and a father in India. You love both of them as truly as a son can love. But the question may arise as to which of them you are to visit or to stay with. Are you to remain in Scotland or go to India? *Love* cannot determine this question, for you love both equally. How is it to be decided? By *duty*. You ask, Is it my *duty* to go to my father, or to remain with my mother? If you decided to leave your mother, from a sense of duty, would she doubt your love, and say, I want none of your professions of it? And when you went to India, and told your father that it was a sense of duty that brought you to him, would he scorn you, and say, I want none of your duty, give me your love?

Duty is a right and proper motive. It is again and

again referred to in Scripture, as the words 'ought,' 'are bound,' 'must,' 'debtor,' 'owe,' and the like, abundantly show. 'He that saith he abideth in Him, *ought* himself so to walk even as He walked' (*1 John 2, v. 6*).

We read such passages as the following:— 'Ye also *ought* to wash one another's feet' (*John 13, v. 14*); — 'We have done that which was our *duty* to do' (*Luke 17, v. 10*); — 'We that are strong *ought* to bear the infirmities of the weak' (*Rom. 15, v. 1*); — 'So *ought* men to love their wives' (*Eph. 5, v. 28*); — 'We are *bound* to thank God' (*2 Thess. 1, v. 3*); — 'We are *bound* to give thanks' (*2 Thess. 2, v. 13*); — 'We *ought* to lay down our lives for the brethren' (*1 John 3, v. 16*); — 'We *ought* to love one another' (*1 John 4, v. 11*). These are a few out of many passages in which *duty* is spoken of in very plain terms. That duty and love should go together, is no proof that there is no such thing as *duty*, or that a Christian should rise above it into the region of 'pure love,' as Romish mystics have held. *Duty* means the thing that is *due*; are we not to do it because it is *due*, because it is the *right* and *proper* thing? Let us exercise our common sense, and understand the meaning of words, whether Greek or English, before soaring into transcendental regions, into which neither prophets nor apostles have gone before us.

There is a danger of running to excess in our day, — of attempting the superfine in religion; of soaring too high, of getting away from both Scripture and common sense; of indulging in a *sentimentalism*, which looks *very* spiritual, but which, when analysed, is simply absurdity, or, at the best, a one-sided exaggeration of some isolated truth. There is great danger, in a time of spiritual quickening, of being carried about with diverse and strange doctrines. Let us cleave to the word. Only thus can we find stedfastness and sobriety. Only by feeding on it, and being guided by it, can we maintain a manly and healthy religion, — free from error, yet devoid of effeminacy, following out the old paths of reformers, apostles, prophets, and patriarchs, unshaken by novelties, yet unfettered by bigotry or self-will.

'He that is dead,' says the apostle, 'is freed from sin' (*Rom. 6, v. 7*); or more exactly, 'He that has died is justified from sin.' Death was the penalty, and he who has paid the penalty is legally justified. There is no further claim against him. We pay the penalty when we take the death of the substitute as ours, and God reckons the penalty paid when He obtains our consent to the exchange. It is the thought of having paid the penalty that pacifies the conscience; and it is the thought of God reckoning it paid that gives us peace with Him. When we come to understand the meaning and value of the work upon the cross; when we accept what God has declared concerning all who believe His testimony to that work, the burden drops, and we enter into liberty.

With that liberty comes holiness. We seek henceforth conformity to Him who has set us free, and who bids us follow Him in the path of conformity to the Father's will.

With that liberty comes love, — love to Him who hath brought our souls out of prison by going into prison for us.

With that love comes zeal, — the zeal of Him who followed after His lost ones till He had recovered them,

— of Him who said, 'The zeal of Thine house hath eaten me up.'

With this love and zeal there comes self-denial, — the self-denial of Him who 'pleased not Himself', — who lived on earth solely for others; though rich, for our sakes becoming poor.

Of all this be it ever remembered, that the root is 'peace with God through our Lord Jesus Christ;' and that this peace comes from the knowledge of the peace-making blood, the blood of the one divine peace-offering, whom to know is peace! It is out of the sacrificial blood that we extract the peace which is the beginning of all service, all religion, all uprightness of walk. 'No condemnation' commences the life of freedom and self-denial and zeal. We cease to know the law as our enemy, and begin to know it as our friend; for that which is 'holy and just and good' must ever be our delight, our joy, our guide. 'I *delight* in the *law* of God after the inner man' (*Rom. 7, v. 22*) is one of our truest watchwords; for we were set free from the law just in order that we might *delight* in the *law* and in order that 'the righteousness of *the law* might be *fulfilled* in us' (*Rom. 8, v. 4*). With law satisfied, — nay, transformed into a friend, and speaking not condemnation, but pardon, not wrath, but love, we walk onwards and upwards, realizing in that blessed law what David did when he said, 'The statutes of the Lord are right, rejoicing the heart. More to be desired are they than gold, yea, than much fine gold: sweeter also than honey, and the honey-comb' (*Ps. 19, vv. 8-10*).